China

by Susan Sinnott

Content Adviser: Professor Sherry L. Field,
Department of Social Science Education, College of Education,
The University of Georgia

Reading Adviser: Dr. Linda D. Labbo,
Department of Reading Education, College of Education,
The University of Georgia

 COMPASS POINT BOOKS

Minneapolis, Minnesota

FIRST REPORTS

Compass Point Books
3722 West 50th Street, #115
Minneapolis, MN 55410

Visit Compass Point Books on the Internet at *www.compasspointbooks.com* or e-mail your
request to *custserv@compasspointbooks.com*

Photographs ©:

FPG International/Keren Su, cover; Photo Network/Bachmann, 4; FPG International/Telegraph Colour Library, 6; Unicorn Stock
Photos/Jeff Greenberg, 7, 8; Corbis/Charles & Josette Lenars, 9; Unicorn Stock Photos/Joe Sohm, 10; North Wind Picture Archives, 12;
Visuals Unlimited/Fritz Polking, 13; North Wind Picture Archives, 14; Archive Photos, 15; North Wind Picture Archives, 16; Archive
Photos/Popperfoto, 17; North Wind Picture Archives, 18; AP/WideWorld/Mark Avery, 19; International Stock/Donna Carroll, 20; Index
Stock Imagery, 22; Visuals Unlimited/Ken Wagner, 23; Unicorn Stock Photos/ChromoSohm/Sohm, 24; International Stock Photo/Tom
Till, 25; International Stock Photo/Loek Polders, 26; Visuals Unlimited/Bill Kamin, 27; International Stock Photo/Stan Ries, 28; Visuals
Unlimited/Steve McCutcheon, 29; Visuals Unlimited/Charles Preitner, 30; International Stock Photo/Johan Elbers, 32; Unicorn Stock
Photos/Florent Flipper, 33; International Stock Photo/Michael Ventura, 34; Visuals Unlimited/Bill Kamin, 35; FPG International/Terry
Qing, 36; Index Stock Imagery/Keren Su, 38; Corbis/Nik Wheeler, 39; Unicorn Stock Photos/Florent Flipper, 40; Corbis/Jack Fields, 41;
Index Stock Imagery/Keren Su, 42.

Editors: E. Russell Primm and Emily J. Dolbear
Photo Researcher: Svetlana Zhurkina
Photo Selector: Dawn Friedman
Design: Bradfordesign, Inc.
Cartography: XNR Productions, Inc.

Library of Congress Cataloging-in-Publication Data

Sinnott, Susan.
   China / by Susan Sinnott.
      p. cm. — (First reports)
   Includes bibliographical references and index.
   Summary: An introduction to the geography, history, culture, and people of China.
   ISBN 0-7565-0029-X (lib. binding)
      1. China—Juvenile literature. [1. China.] I. Title. II. Series.
   DS706 .S5 2000
   951—dc21   00-008525

Table of Contents

"Ni hao!"

Ni hao! "Good day! Welcome to China!"

You might hear this greeting if you visit China. China touches fourteen other countries in East Asia. Russia lies to the north, Pakistan to the west, India and Nepal to the south, and the Pacific Ocean to the east. China's highest peak is Mount Everest, at 29,028 feet (8,854 meters). It is also the highest mountain in the world. Many climbers have died trying to reach the top of Mount Everest.

▲ *A Chinese woman in traditional costume*

▲ *Map of China*

About 2,000 years ago, the Chinese thought their country was at the center of the world. They called it *Chung Kuo*, or "Middle Kingdom." Its capital, Chang'an (now the city of Xian), was the world's largest city.

▲ *Most people in Beijing travel by bicycle.*

Today, more than 1 billion people live in China. This is more people than in any other country. Its capital and largest city is Beijing.

▲ *Highways and apartment buildings in the crowded capital city of Beijing*

The Teachings of Confucius

▲ *A statue of the Chinese teacher named Confucius*

Long ago, small states in China were always at war with one another. In about 500 B.C., a teacher named Confucius felt that people should practice kindness, respect, and duty—not hatred and selfishness. He felt that China's rulers should set an example, just as parents do for their children. His beliefs came to be called Confucianism.

The teachings of Confucius helped bring China's first emperor to power in 221 B.C. Finally, China had one leader and one government. The system worked so well for China that it lasted until 1912!

Still, the great Chinese Empire had many enemies in the north and the south. To keep out these enemies, the emperor, named Shi Huangdi of the Qin dynasty, had a wall built around parts of the country.

▲ *China's first emperor began building the Great Wall.*

▲ *China's Great Wall*

The Great Wall was so big that it took millions of workers hundreds of years to finish. Some parts of the wall are 20 feet (6 meters) high and so wide that ten soldiers could walk on it side by side.

Even today, it snakes through more than 4,000 miles (6,436 kilometers) of desert and mountainous areas in northern China. It is the only man-made structure that can be seen with the naked eye from the moon.

The Silk Road

▲ *Making silk in the early days of China*

Before 100 B.C., the people of Europe and the Middle East and the Chinese did not know about one another. All that changed when a soft, beautiful cloth called silk was traded from **merchant** to merchant all the way from China to Rome. Silk quickly became popular among wealthy Romans. Pure silk was more valuable than China's paper, printing, and gunpowder.

Traders from the Chinese capital loaded silk on camels and set off to trade with the western merchants. This **ancient** route, called the Silk Road, crossed mountains and deserts. It stretched about 4,000 miles (6,436 km). The silk changed hands several times before reaching the Mediterranean Sea.

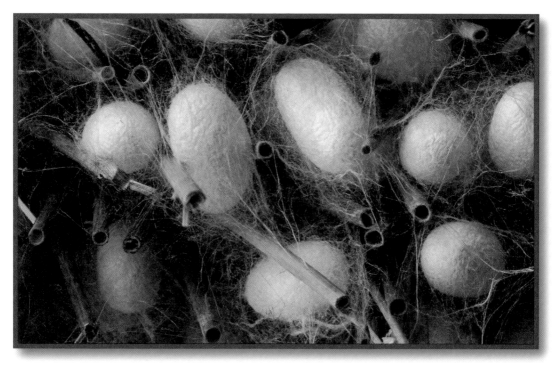

▲ Silk is woven from silkworm cocoons.

▲ *Traders traveling on the Silk Road*

There, merchants from China met traders from Syria and Persia. The Chinese traded silk for fine metal-work, glass, and gold coins. Over time, ideas were traded too.

Soon people on the Silk Road were passing on the words of an ancient Indian holy man called

▲ *The Buddha, an ancient Indian holy man*

the Buddha. His teachings became a religion called Buddhism. Before long, Buddhism became one of China's major religions.

By around A.D. 400, the Silk Road was not used as much. But in 1271, an Italian traveler named Marco Polo left his home in Venice to visit China. He traveled east along the Silk Road.

When Marco Polo finally arrived in China three years later, the great leader Kublai Khan of nearby Mongolia

▲ An Italian named Marco Polo traveled the Silk Road in 1271.

▲ *Marco Polo is welcomed to the court of Kublai Khan.*

▲ The great Mongolian leader Kublai Khan

ruled the Chinese Empire. Marco Polo worked for
Kublai Khan's government for seventeen years. When
he returned to Italy, he wrote a book about his years
in China, but no one believed his tales. The Mongols
were forced out of China in 1368.

Opening Its Doors

In the centuries that followed, China opened its doors to the rest of the world only a crack. And it often slammed those doors shut again.

The last Chinese emperor gave up his throne in 1912. For the first time, the Chinese people elected their own government. But then, in 1949, a new government that forced people to support **Communism** took over. Communism is a political system in which the government owns almost everything.

▲ *In 1999, Chinese president Jiang Zemin opened his country's doors wider on his first state visit to Australia.*

▲ This portrait of Mao Zedong, leader of Communist China, hangs in Tiananmen Square.

Forty years later, students marched in Beijing's Tiananmen Square. They were protesting the lack of freedom in China. Chinese troops killed hundreds of students in the Tiananmen Square Massacre. *Tiananmen* means "the Gate of Heavenly Peace." Many people around the world spoke out against the Chinese government after the Tiananmen Square Massacre.

▲ *Student protesters in Tiananmen Square*

The Three Ways

Taoism, Confucianism, and Buddhism are China's major religions. They are sometimes called "the three ways." Taoism is based on the teachings of Lao Zi, who lived a few hundred years before Confucius. Taoists believe that people must live in harmony with nature.

Today, a trip to any Chinese temple shows the visitor how the three major religions have mixed over the centuries. Statues of gods fill the rooms and halls. They represent good

▲ This temple in Beijing is called the Temple of Heaven.

▲ *These stone lions guard a temple's doors.*

health, riches, or long life. Two large stone lions called door gods always stand silent guard against evil spirits. Once inside the temple, people worshipping the Buddha light pieces of paper to offer thanks or show respect for loved ones.

There are also many statues of the Buddha. He is often shown as plump and kindly. People often rub the belly of a Buddha statue for good luck.

Language

Most Chinese speak *Putonghua*, or Mandarin. The language has many variations, or **dialects**. The dialects differ from one part of the country to another. Sometimes there are even differences from one village to another!

All the dialects are written the same way though. Mandarin Chinese has up to 50,000 letters written as tiny pictures, or **characters**. There are only 400 different sounds. The sounds can be hard to understand from one dialect to another, but the words are the same.

▲ *Chinese letters carved into a mossy rock*

Chinese Art

▲ *A Chinese artist stitches colorful nature scenes onto silk.*

When a traditional artist in China paints a picture, it happens very fast. The artist does not need to look at a real bug to paint one. Artists in China paint from memory. They usually paint flowers or trees. They also paint birds, animals, fish, or people. When they paint a picture, they use a pointed brush. Chinese artists always paint on silk or paper. Their paints are made from plants or minerals.

Calligraphy is another art form in China. For many thousands of years, only artists could paint the delicate strokes of the characters used in the Chinese language. The art of painting or drawing words with ink is called calligraphy. Only four tools are used in Chinese calligraphy—brush,

▲ *A traditional Chinese painter*

▲ A calligrapher at work

ink stick, ink stone, and paper. They are called "the four treasures." The Chinese often hang poems or traditional sayings written in fine calligraphy on their walls.

In the seventh century, the Chinese discovered fine white clay along the banks of the Yellow and

▲ *White clay from the banks of the Yantze River was used to make fine dishes.*

▲ Painting china dishes by hand is an art form in China.

Yangtze Rivers. They found they could shape the clay into plates and bowls as thin as eggshells. Artists painted designs, often in blue, on the dishes and traded them with western merchants. These fine-art pieces were popular in the Middle East and Europe. There, the dishes were called simply "china."

The Opera

Chinese, or Beijing, opera is nothing like western operas. Chinese opera singers do not simply perform musically. They are also dancers, acrobats, and mimes.

The first Chinese operas took place on city streets. Performers banged on gongs, cymbals, and drums to attract attention. Today, in grand theaters in China, each performance still begins with this mixture of harsh sounds.

▲ Performers in Beijing opera wear fancy costumes.

Then the actors, with painted faces and colorful flowing robes, take the stage and tell familiar folk stories. An orchestra of traditional Chinese instruments plays at most opera performances.

Children love to spend an evening at the opera. The audience often shouts back to the performers, especially when their favorite character, the Monkey King, takes the stage.

▲ *Students at the Central School of Beijing Opera in Beijing*

▲ A Chinese chef makes noodles by hand.

Food in China

Food is an important part of Chinese life. When Chinese people eat meals together, they sit close to one another at a low table. A meal never begins until everyone is seated. The oldest are served first. Everyone eats with chopsticks.

Mandarin, Szechwan, and Cantonese are the main kinds of Chinese food, and they are all favorites around the world. They use the freshest vegetables, chicken, fish, and spices. Most dishes are served with rice.

▲ The Chinese take food preparation seriously.

▲ *A farmer works in the rice fields, or paddies.*

After all, China is the world's biggest producer of rice. At meals, children are urged to eat every grain. Leaving a bowl spotted with rice grains, parents warn, brings bad luck.

The Chinese believe that all food and drink affects the body's energy and balance. They are careful not to serve many spicy foods, cold foods, or foods with the same color and texture at once. The Chinese are true artists in the kitchen!

Chinese Festivals

▲ Children and lion dancers celebrate the Chinese New Year.

Gung hay fat choi! means "May you have good fortune and happiness!" This greeting begins the Chinese New Year. Depending on the Chinese moon calendar, the festival usually starts in late January and ends in late February.

▲ *A boy sets off firecrackers for the New Year celebration.*

Families travel great distances to be together for New Year's Eve. At midnight, people pour into the streets and set off firecrackers to chase away evil spirits.

On the first day of the New Year, children visit their older relatives and are given a small red envelope with paper money. The celebration ends with a parade and more firecrackers.

Later in the day, a colorful dragon made from paper, silk, and bamboo is carried through the city streets. The dragon looks like it is dancing! The New Year in China is a very festive holiday.

▲ People lead a paper dragon through the city streets on New Year's Day.

▲ *A dragon kite for the Festival of Ascending on High*

The first nine days of September are a holiday called the Festival of Ascending on High. For this festival, schoolchildren make kites and fly them. There is no school on the last day of the festival and children fly their kites all day. As evening falls, they let their

▲ *The panda bear has become an international symbol for the country of China.*

kites sail away with the wind, taking bad luck, sickness, and evil spirits with them. Only happiness is left behind.

If you visit China, you will learn more about this huge and interesting country. Then as you leave, you will probably say, "*Xie xie!* Thank you! I enjoyed my visit to China."

Glossary

ancient—very old

calligraphy—the art of painting or drawing Chinese characters with ink

characters—letters written as tiny pictures

Communism—a political system in which the government owns almost everything

dialects—variations in a language

merchant—a trader

Did You Know?

- The Chinese have made kites out of bamboo and paper or silk for thousands of years.

- The Chinese believe the color red brings good luck.

- There are 9,999 rooms in the Imperial Palace buildings in the Forbidden City.

At a Glance

Official name: *Zhonghua Renmin Gongheguo* (People's Republic of China)

Capital: Beijing

Official language(s): Northern Chinese Mandarin or Putonghua

National song: "March of the Volunteers"

Area: 3,695,000 square miles (9,570,050 square kilometers)

Highest point: Mount Everest, 29,028 feet (8,854 meters) above sea level

Lowest point: Turpan Pendi (Turfan Depression), 505 feet (154 meters) below sea level

Population: 1,236,914,658 (1998 estimate)

Head of government: Premier

Money: Yuan

Important Dates

500 B.C. Confucius teaches kindness, respect, and duty.

100 B.C. Merchants begin to travel the Silk Road from China to Rome.

221 B.C. Shi Huangdi of the Qin dynasty becomes emperor with a strong central government.

A.D. 400 The Silk Road is no longer used.

1368 The Mongols are forced out of China.

1912 The Chinese government is elected for the first time.

1949 A Communist government takes over in China.

1989 Hundreds of students are killed in Beijing's Tiananmen Square.

Want to Know More?

At the Library

Dramer, Kim. *People's Republic of China*. Danbury, Conn.: Children's Press, 1999.

So, Sungwan. *C Is for China*. Parsippany, N.J.: Silver Press, 1998.

Steele, Philip. *Step into the Chinese Empire*. New York: Lorenz Books, 1998.

On the Web

China Today
http://www.chinatoday.com/
For details and current news about China and its culture

Discovering China
http://library.thinkquest.org/26469/
For information about the history of China, its people, its cities, and the country's cultural contributions

Through the Mail

Chinese Embassy
2300 Connecticut Avenue, N.W.
Washington, DC 20008
For information about China

On the Road

China National Tourist Office
350 Fifth Avenue, Suite 6413
Empire State Building
New York, NY 10118
212/760-8218
To find out about visiting China

Index

About the Author

Susan Sinnott has written two books in the American Girl Collection by the Pleasant Company. She has also written for Children's Press, Franklin Watts, and Millbrook Press and contributed to *Cobblestone* and *Cricket* magazines. Her *Extraordinary Hispanic Americans* was chosen as an ALA Best Reference Book of 1993. Susan Sinnott lives with her two children in Maine.